A Note to Parents

DK READERS is a compelling program for beginning readers, designed in conjunction with leading literacy experts, including Dr. Linda Gambrell, Professor of Education at Clemson University. Dr. Gambrell has served as President of the National Reading Conference, the College Reading Association, and the International Reading Association.

Beautiful illustrations and superb full-color photographs combine with engaging, easy-to-read stories to offer a fresh approach to each subject in the series. Each DK READER is guaranteed to capture a child's interest while developing his or her reading skills, general knowledge, and love of reading.

The five levels of DK READERS are aimed at different reading abilities, enabling you to choose the books that are exactly right for your child:

Pre-level 1: Learning to read
Level 1: Beginning to read
Level 2: Beginning to read alone
Level 3: Reading alone
Level 4: Proficient readers

The "normal" age at which a child begins to read can be anywhere from three to eight years old. Adult participation through the lower levels is very helpful for providing encouragement, discussing storylines, and sounding out unfamiliar words.

No matter which level you select, you can be sure that you are helping your child learn to read, then read to learn!

LONDON, NEW YORK, MUNICH,
MELBOURNE, AND DELHI

For DK/Brady Games
Publisher David Waybright
Editor-in-chief H. Leigh Davis
Licensing Director Mike Degler
International Translations Brian Saliba
Director of Business Development
Michael Vaccaro
Title Manager Tim Fitzpatrick

Reading Consultant
Linda B. Gambrell, Ph.D.

Produced by
Shoreline Publishing Group LLC
President James Buckley Jr.
Designer Tom Carling, carlingdesign.com

For WWE
Director, Home Entertainment & Books
Dean Miller
Photo Department
Frank Vitucci, Joshua Tottenham, Jamie Nelsen
Copy Editor Kevin Caldwell
Legal Lauren Dienes-Middlen

First American Edition, 2009
10 11 10 9 8 7 6 5 4 3 2
Published in the United States by DK Publishing
375 Hudson Street, New York, New York 10014

DK books are available at special discounts when purchased in bulk
for sales promotions, premiums, fund-raising, or educational use.
For details, contact: DK Publishing Special Markets,
375 Hudson Street, New York, New York 10014
SpecialSales@dk.com

A catalog record for this book is available
from the Library of Congress.

ISBN: 978-0-7566-5385-9 (Paperback)
ISBN: 978-0-7566-5386-6 (Hardcover)

Printed and bound by Lake Book

The publisher would like to thank the following for their kind
permission to reproduce their photographs:
All photos courtesy WWE Entertainment, Inc.
All other images © Dorling Kindersley
For further information see: www.dkimages.com

Discover more at
www.dk.com

Contents

DK **READERS**

READING
3
ALONE

Undertaker®

Written by Kevin Sullivan

DK

DK Publishing

A figure in black

On a cold November night in 1990, a menacing figure dressed in black made his way toward the ring at the WWE *Survivor Series.* A hush fell over the sold-out Hartford Civic Center, as fans and WWE Superstars struggled to understand what they were seeing. Never before had such a mysterious man stepped into a WWE ring. He stood nearly seven feet tall (3.1 m) and weighed close to 300 pounds (136 kg).

The bell rang, launching the match and the career of this giant of a man. He quickly showed an astonishing combination of speed and power. His opponents that night—Koko B. Ware, Dusty Rhodes, and The Hart Foundation—were stunned.

Undertaker took care of Dusty Rhodes with no trouble.

Within a minute, the man in the trench coat, black hat, gray boots, and gloves took out Koko B. Ware with what would soon become his signature move, the "Tombstone Piledriver." Dusty Rhodes went down next, in nearly the same amount of time. The match was over almost as soon as it began.

The crowd erupted, thrilled by the huge figure in the ring.

Undertaker had arrived.

WWE would never be the same again.

In time, he would go on to win every major championship in WWE competition—some more than once. He would rack up an astonishing 17–0 record in *WrestleMania*, a record unmatched in WWE history. But that night in Hartford, Undertaker's story had only just begun.

Undertaker's Stats and Stuff
- Height: 6' 10 ½ " (2.1 m)
- Weight: 299 lbs. (136 kg)
- From: Death Valley
- Finishing Moves: Chokeslam, Tombstone Piledriver, Last Ride

The beginning

Very little is known about the origin of this dark figure. He goes by many names, including "The Deadman." In fact, it's said he comes from Death Valley itself.

During his long WWE career, he has strangely disappeared for months. Many thought that he was dead or had returned to whatever mysterious place he was from. But he has always come back to the ring, to menace and overpower all his foes.

Even when Undertaker is defeated in the ring, he always returns. From the grave? From beyond? No one knows for sure. But one thing is certain: Few other WWE Superstars strike as much fear into the hearts of their ring opponents.

The sound of a gong signals Undertaker's arrival.

From the moment he first stepped
into the ring, Undertaker took WWE by
storm. Using the devastating force of his
Tombstone Piledriver, he quickly laid

*Undertaker's entry into the arena always brings a thrill to
his many fans.*

Undertaker's Nicknames

- The Phenom
- The Deadman
- Big Evil
- The Demon from Death Valley
- The Lord of Darkness

waste to many of WWE's top Superstars. His first big-time match came at *WrestleMania VII*. His opponent was the legendary Jimmy "Superfly" Snuka. Not the least bit intimidated by his WWE Hall of Fame opponent, Undertaker stared deep into the eyes of "Superfly." The Deadman worked with great speed and power to quickly defeat Snuka—in less than five minutes! The victory was the first of what would eventually become the most impressive *WrestleMania* record in WWE history.

Hulk Hogan felt the powerful wrath of Undertaker!

A WWE Champion

One year after making his amazing debut, Undertaker returned to *Survivor Series* with a new goal: the WWE Championship. In his way stood Hulk Hogan, one of the greatest Superstars in WWE history. But nothing bothered "The Lord of Darkness," not even facing someone with the Hulkster's impressive achievements.

By night's end, Undertaker had defeated the popular Hogan to capture his first WWE Championship. It would not be his last.

Undertaker's first reign as champ was short, however. A week later, on *Tuesday in Texas*, he battled Hogan again with the title on the line. Undertaker couldn't hold off Hogan a second time, and he gave back the title amid controversy. Despite the loss, greatness was still ahead.

Undertaker's WWE History

- Undefeated at *WrestleMania*
- WWE Champion
- World Heavyweight Champion
- WWE Hardcore Champion
- World Tag Team Champion

Undertaker's first WWE Championship not only made him a main-event Superstar, it also put a permanent target on his back. Everyone wanted to defeat Undertaker.

The 380-pound "Ugandan Giant" Kamala, as well as the near eight-foot Giant Gonzales, were the first gigantic men to try. Despite their size, neither could beat the "Phenom." Undertaker turned back the Ugandan Giant at *SummerSlam 1992*, and again in the first-ever Coffin Match at *Survivor Series* in 1992. He then twice chopped Giant Gonzales down to size.

Coffin Match
A match in which a coffin is placed in or just outside the ring. The first combatant to place his opponent inside the coffin wins the match.

Undertaker refused to lose to the mighty Giant Gonzales.

Heading into 1994, Undertaker appeared impossible to stop. Then he ran into a 600-pound wall known as Yokozuna and his gang of thugs at the 1994 *Royal Rumble*. With Bam Bam Bigelow, Crush, Diesel, and many others helping, Yokozuna stuffed the "Deadman" into a ringside casket.

Once he was sealed inside the casket, fans wondered if they would ever see Undertaker again. Then something very strange happened. His spirit appeared on the arena's giant video screen, speaking to the stunned crowd from inside the casket. He warned those who defeated him that he would return.

Undertaker's spirit appears on the giant video screen.

And then he did something even
stranger; he dropped completely out of
sight. WWE fans waited for the next
move in this mysterious journey.

Undertaker vs. Undertaker

Much of 1994 passed with no sign of the "Deadman." He didn't even appear at *WrestleMania*, which had become his signature event. With each passing month, fans began to wonder if they

Undertaker depended on his manager, Paul Bearer, to help him take on foes in and out of the ring.

would ever see the amazing Undertaker again. Then, from an unexpected source, a glimmer of hope appeared.

The well-known and much-disliked WWE manager Ted DiBiase announced that he had found the missing Undertaker. Fans began to grow excited at the thought of seeing their hero again. But Paul Bearer, Undertaker's manager, wasn't buying DiBiase's story.

Bearer also claimed to have found the lost fan favorite. How could this be? They couldn't both be right. Two different men claimed to be Undertaker. One was obviously faking it. What could be done to solve this mysterious problem? A battle, of course. After all, this is WWE!

Confident they both had the real Undertaker, DiBiase and Bearer agreed to have their men battle at *SummerSlam 1994*. The winner would be declared the true "Deadman." Stepping into the ring, both men certainly looked like Undertaker. But when the fighting began, the "Phenom" proved just who he was.

In the end, Bearer's Undertaker nailed DiBiase's fake—called "Underfaker" by fans—with three Tombstone Piledrivers. The real Undertaker had been revealed. More importantly to WWE fans, he was back!

Undertaker's Famous Moves
- Chokeslam
- Tombstone Piledriver
- Last Ride
- Corner Clothesline
- Old School
- Sidewalk Slam

Underfaker vs. Undertaker . . . or the other way around?

Embarrassed by the loss, DiBiase brought in others to try their hand at beating Undertaker. Just as the Underfaker had done, they all failed miserably.

Ted DiBiase's WWE Superstars still wanted to beat Undertaker. They made their first attempt at *WrestleMania XI*. That's where DiBiase gained some revenge when his "Supreme Fighting Machine" Kama stole Undertaker's ever-present, power-giving urn. Adding insult to injury, Kama later melted down the urn and transformed it into a necklace he wore with great pride.

With the mystical urn no longer by his side, many questioned whether Undertaker could maintain his dominance. The "Phenom's" fans,

Undertaker's Urn

From the beginning of his WWE career, Undertaker was always seen carrying an urn of the type used to carry the ashes of the dead. Undertaker claimed that he drew mystical power from the urn, giving him strength during his matches.

known as the "Creatures of the Night,"
were there to help him through this
darkest period. Fueled by the support of
his Creatures, Undertaker gained the
ultimate revenge when he defeated
Kama in a Casket
Match at
*SummerSlam
1995.*

Enter Mankind

In 1996, WWE opened its doors to one of the most bizarre personalities in its history. Known simply as Mankind, this super-strange Superstar was often spotted sitting in dark boiler rooms, rocking back and forth while ranting to his pet rat, George. Mankind's weirdness put off just about everyone, and few people wanted to battle him.

In fact, only one WWE Superstar was bold enough to step into the ring with such an odd individual. That man was, of course, Undertaker. Over the next several years, the two Superstars engaged in one of the most

Mankind tried to beat Undertaker in this 1996 match.

heated rivalries in WWE history. Their
feud became so intense that it led to the
creation of two new types of matches:
the Boiler Room Brawl and the Buried
Alive Match.

At *SummerSlam 1996*, Undertaker had the odds stacked against him more than he even realized. He agreed to face Mankind in a Boiler Room Brawl—a type of match that clearly favored Mankind, who spent his free time

Manager Paul Bearer turned against Undertaker.

hanging out in boiler rooms! But he also had to deal with an unexpected opponent: Paul Bearer.

Undertaker's longtime friend and manager stunned WWE when he struck the "Deadman" with his own urn. This shocking move not only gave Mankind the edge he needed to pick up the win, but it also marked the end to one of the most successful partnerships of all time.

After this news-making event, the Undertaker-Mankind rivalry continued to thrill WWE fans.

Undertaker appeared to get his revenge for the boiler room betrayal when he defeated Mankind in a Buried Alive Match in October 1996. But the celebration was short lived. After being declared the victor, the "Phenom" was attacked by the masked Executioner. Mankind and Executioner then teamed up to bury the "Deadman" alive under a mound of dirt. Unbelievably, however, Undertaker managed to survive the burial. Then, the following month, he completed his revenge when he defeated Mankind at *Survivor Series.*

Building on the momentum from his rivalry and from his victories over Mankind, Undertaker went on to defeat WWE Superstars Faarooq and Crush. This impressive string of wins led to the "Phenom" being named the number one contender for the WWE Championship.

Undertaker arranged for the end of Mankind!

More than five years after losing the celebrated title, Undertaker beat Sycho Sid at *WrestleMania 13* to recapture the WWE Championship. But unlike his first WWE Championship reign, Undertaker held a strong grasp on the title for close to five months. During his reign, he successfully turned back such WWE Superstars as the British Bulldog, Stone Cold Steve Austin, and Vader.

However, an accident brought down the "Deadman." At *SummerSlam 1997*, guest referee and WWE Superstar Shawn Michaels accidentally nailed the champ with a chair. The blow dropped Undertaker to the mat long enough for Bret "Hit Man" Hart to win and take the title away.

Undertaker faced down Sycho Sid to win the title again.

Brothers of Destruction

After losing the WWE Championship in such disappointing fashion, Undertaker set out to take his revenge on Shawn

Competitors battle inside or outside a giant steel cage.

Michaels. Defeating Michaels in a traditional one-on-one contest would not be good enough for the "Phenom." The two squared off at *Badd Blood* inside a giant steel cage.

Undertaker appeared to be getting his revenge. But before he could put the finishing touches on Michaels, the "Deadman" got the biggest shock of his life. He came face to face with Kane, his long-lost half-brother!

For decades, Undertaker didn't know whether Kane was dead or alive. According to Bearer, Kane had disappeared in a mysterious fire long ago. Now Kane had returned and he wanted to battle Undertaker.

Kane ripped down the cage to get at Undertaker.

In the months that followed, Undertaker refused to battle Kane. But when Kane attacked the "Phenom" at the 1998 *Royal Rumble*, Undertaker had little choice but to respond with force. They finally agreed to settle their family feud at *WrestleMania XIV*.

After an emotional back-and-forth battle, Undertaker walked away with the win, although it took three Tombstone Piledrivers to take down Kane. The match marked the beginning of a rollercoaster relationship for the two. They competed against each other

Inferno Matches
In the dangerous and difficult Inferno Matches, live flames surround the ring. The combatants must duel amid the fire! They have to avoid their opponent's big moves along with hot flames!

The end of another successful Tombstone Piledriver!

in Inferno Matches, but also teamed up
long enough to capture both the World
and WCW Tag Team Championships.

Undertaker and his followers, the Ministry of Darkness.

Ministry of Darkness

After years as a WWE fan favorite Superstar, Undertaker made the unpopular decision to get back together with manager Paul Bearer in 1999. With a darker-than-ever attitude, the "Deadman" began to gather his WWE disciples into what he called his "Ministry of Darkness." His top recruits included

Viscera, Mideon, the Acolytes, and the Brood.

Undertaker and his Ministry unleashed a devastating onslaught on all of WWE. While anybody in WWE was a target, their chief victim was Mr. McMahon's daughter, Stephanie. In April 1999, Undertaker planned to marry her in a bizarre wedding ceremony. However, the "Deadman's" devious plans went up in smoke when Stone Cold Steve Austin saved the reluctant bride from Undertaker's clutches. The following month, Undertaker gained the ultimate revenge by not only defeating Stone Cold, but capturing his WWE Championship, too. The victory marked the third time at the top of WWE for the "Phenom."

After a brief break, Undertaker returned to the ring in May 2000. This time, though, the successful Superstar traded in his "Deadman" image for a completely different look. Riding into the *Judgment Day* event on a custom motorcycle, Undertaker was now a biker with a bad attitude.

Even with his new look, Undertaker continued to dominate inside the ring. He defeated such Superstars as The Rock, Kurt Angle, and Chris Jericho. He even topped Triple H at *WrestleMania X-Seven* and Ric Flair at *WrestleMania X8* to improve his impressive *WrestleMania* record to 10-0.

In May 2002, more than a decade after defeating Hulk Hogan for his first WWE Championship, Undertaker challenged the Hulkster yet again for the same prize at *Judgment Day*. Once again, Undertaker put an end to Hogan's championship reign.

A new look for Undertaker, complete with motorcycle!

The Deadman rises

For the next two months, Undertaker proudly rode to the ring with the WWE Championship strapped around his waist. Then in July 2002, The Rock defeated him and Kurt Angle in a

Angle's got The Rock . . . and here comes Undertaker!

Triple Threat Match
This is a three-way match in which three Superstars battle it out, with the last man standing declared the winner.

Triple Threat Match to claim the title. That was not all Undertaker had to deal with. The on-again, off-again battle between Undertaker and Kane flared up in late 2003.

The "Big Red Monster" (Kane's nickname) helped Mr. McMahon defeat Undertaker in a Buried Alive Match at *Survivor Series 2003.* Kane tossed mounds of dirt over Undertaker's body, leaving many fans believing that they would never see their hero again.

Buried under dirt? No problem for Undertaker!

Proving you can't kill what's already dead, Undertaker made his highly anticipated return to WWE at

WrestleMania XX. Returning to the "Deadman" look that had made him so popular in the past, he defeated Kane to keep his *WrestleMania* record perfect at an amazing 12-0.

The following year, a young and rising WWE Superstar named Randy Orton was bold enough to try his hand at stopping Undertaker's unprecedented *WrestleMania* streak. But, like all the others, he too ultimately fell to the mystical force of the "Phenom."

Further proving his greatness, Undertaker continued to dominate Orton in the months that followed. This included a victory at *Armageddon 2005*, where he defeated the brash youngster in an always-intense steel cell match.

By 2007, Undertaker had achieved just about everything possible in WWE. However, he still had never won a *Royal Rumble* or captured the coveted World Heavyweight Championship.

Undertaker took care of the first in January 2007 when he eliminated Shawn Michaels to win his first *Royal Rumble* match. Then he used his Tombstone Piledriver to beat the "Animal" and capture his first World Heavyweight Championship.

In 2009, in front of more than 72,000 screaming fans at *The 25th Anniversary of WrestleMania*, Undertaker held off Shawn Michaels, using his patented Tombstone Piledriver to seal another victory. Through 2009, Undertaker's *WrestleMania* record stands at an amazing 17-0.

Shawn Michaels became another Undertaker victim!

Outside the ring, Undertaker disappears from view. While some WWE Superstars can be seen in movies or on TV shows, Undertaker vanishes. Does he go to the land of the dead? No one knows . . . and no one is brave enough to ask!

With nearly two decades at the top of WWE to his credit, Undertaker has set an unmatched record during his long run. Along the way, he has captured the hearts of WWE fans, while at the same time striking fear into many of the game's toughest Superstars.

His origins are veiled in mist. His wrestling past is decorated with golden accomplishments. And his future—in and out of the ring—will always remain shrouded in mystery.

Glossary

Anticipated
Looked forward to

Astonishing
Amazing, stunning, surprising

Betrayal
The act of turning your back on someone who trusts you

Brash
Bold, egotistical

Casket
A coffin

Combatant
A fighter, one who battles

Coveted
Desired, hoped for

Debut
Someone's or something's first appearance

Disciple
A person who closely follows and learns from another person

Feud
An ongoing argument or disagreement

Finishing move
The move a Superstar uses to end a match and defeat his or her opponent

Glimmer
A twinkle, a flicker, or a shimmer

Manager
Someone who helps shape and guide a Superstar's career and sets up matches for him or her

Opponent
A rival, foe, or enemy; the person against whom a Superstar competes

Recapture
To get again

Reign
The period of time during which a person holds power

Ring
A square mat surrounded by ropes in which a WWE match takes place

Urn
A vase, pot, jug, or pitcher, often used for holding the ashes of the dead